Questions and

Answers

on Addiction

About the author:

Dr. Wetsman graduated Summa Cum Laude from Tulane University in New Orleans, Louisiana and received his medical degree from Louisiana State University Medical School. He did his internship at the National Naval Medical Center in Bethesda, Maryland. The next few years were spent as a General Medical Officer in the Navy, two of them onboard USS Mount Whitney. After completing a residency in Psychiatry at LSU, Dr Wetsman returned to his uniform at Naval Medical Center, Portsmouth, Virginia where he was active in opening an addiction treatment ward. Returning to New Orleans Dr Wetsman has been active in treating addiction in facilities ranging from inpatient units to Charity Hospital's HIV clinic. He currently serves as Chief Medical Officer of Townsend and is on the board of the American Society of Addiction Medicine (ASAM).

Disclaimer: The contents of this book are the opinions of Dr Wetsman and do not necessarily represent those of Townsend, ASAM or any other organization with which Dr Wetsman is acquainted. This book is intended for educational purposes only. It should not be considered medical advice nor should you act on any of the ideas in this book without first consulting with your own physician.

Questions and Answers

on Addiction

Howard Wetsman MD

Questions and Answers on Addiction

Rush Press
2600 Johnston St.
Suite 110
Lafayette, La 70503

First printing in the United States of America 2007

CIP Data
Wetsman, Howard, 1959-
     Questions and Answers on Addiction / Howard Wetsman --- 1st ed.
     p. cm.
ISBN-13: 978-0-9800891-0-3
ISBN-10: 0-9800891-0-7

     1. Substance abuse—Popular works. 2. Substance abuse—Physiological aspects. 3. Substance abuse—Treatment
     I. Title.
     RC564.29.W48 2007
     616.86
     QB107-600294

Contents

Questions and Answers on Addiction

Dedication

This book is dedicated to all the patients who taught me about addiction.

Preface

This book was inspired by my patients. It was their questions that prompted it and created it.

This book is not intended to be a complete treatment of the disease of addiction. It's also not intended that you read it through from beginning to end. You can if you wish, of course, but you could also just take a look at the contents and pick a question that interests you. Some of the answers refer to information from previous questions and some will stand alone.

There are two main points to this book, so I'll summarize them here. The first is that addiction, not alcoholism or cocaine dependence or compulsive gambling, is the disease that requires medical attention as opposed to any particular behavior patients or their families find troubling. The second is that addiction usually causes symptoms before the troubling behavior started and will continue to cause symptoms after the behavior stops. Putting those two points together has a number of implications, but most important is that people recovering from addiction should be in care for the illness regardless of whether they are using or not; the illness does not go away with the drugs. The new science that has emerged and continues to be discovered tells us that this brain disease is a chronic progressive condition that requires care throughout the life cycle much as does diabetes, asthma, and hypertension. For the past 50 years our focus has been on the drug and the behavior as evidenced by our legal efforts such as the "War Against Drugs." These efforts have largely failed and addiction is, if anything, a bigger rather than smaller problem than it was 50 years ago. New science is showing us a better way to change our society by treating this disease as a disease and giving us, for the first time, effective biological tools. This is a hopeful time for the treatment of addiction, and that hope is what this book is about.

1. Why did you write a book?

Addiction is a subject that brings up a lot of emotions that usually come from what we learned about addiction early in life. Even among people who learned about addiction in school you'll find far more influence on their opinions from what they learned at home than what they learned at school.

What I saw in my patients, who got better and who got worse, was telling me something much different from what I'd learned about addiction in school. The ideas I learned in school didn't seem to fit when the goal was getting people better. The definitions of addiction I had learned didn't seem to be the same ones that my patients were experiencing.

Since what I learned about addiction was not helping many of my patients, I started carefully looking at those patients who were recovering successfully. I noticed something that the successful patients had in common. They had gotten involved in 12-step recovery. It didn't seem to matter what they were addicted to or what 12-step recovery group they went to; the patients who were in 12-step recovery did better as a group than the ones who weren't. So what was it about 12-step recovery that worked? Was it something I could replicate in my work with patients?

About the same time I heard a lecture about the brain's reward system that finally made sense to me. What if addictions weren't different from each other? What if heroin addiction was the same as alcoholism? What if there was a core problem that all my addicted patients had that was the same even though they looked so different from each other on the outside? What if 12-step recovery worked on that core problem and that's why it didn't matter what addiction someone had once they got into recovery?

That's a lot of questions. And it took a lot of reading and time to fit all the pieces of the puzzle together. I may not have everything right, but it makes sense to me. Before, when I followed what I had learned in school, addicts were hard if not impossible to treat. Now it's all I do and it's not so hard. Before, not many people got well. Now I have more success.

Most patients I meet are as confused about this disease as I was. They grew up in the same society I did with the same misconceptions about what addiction is, what it means, and how to live if you have it. So I wrote this book to get the explanation out as far as I could.

I won't say that everything in this book is right. All I can tell you is that it's true for me. With this information my patients do better. Frankly, I'm tired of the academic arguing about who's right and who's wrong. What matters is that people recover and get their lives back.

2. Why call addiction a disease?

Well, first, what's a disease? Here's the answer I got from dictionary.com:

> *a disordered or incorrectly functioning organ, part, structure, or system of the body resulting from the effect of genetic or developmental errors, infection, poisons, nutritional deficiency or imbalance, toxicity, or unfavorable environmental factors; illness; sickness; ailment.*[1]

See that first line, "disordered or incorrectly functioning organ…" That's where the trouble has been all these years. What we see when we look at an addict isn't a broken leg or a fever or a rash; what we see is behavior we don't like. So instead of thinking of addiction as a disease or illness, we've been thinking of it as just a set of behaviors, a moral problem. Even when doctors finally realized it is an illness, most of society couldn't believe it because we couldn't show them the broken organ. Part of what I want to accomplish in this book is to show you the broken organ so that you can understand that addiction is a disease and that it has a good treatment.

---

[1] www.dictionary.com: disease.

3. When did doctors realize addiction is a disease?

Most of this history comes from "Slaying the Dragon,"[2] an excellent book by William White on the history of addiction and its treatment. In 1873, Dr. Charles Hewitt of the Minnesota Board of Health called on the State of Minnesota to declare that "inebriation is a disease; that it demands the same public facilities for its treatment as other diseases." (p.199) And there it stood for many years. Many hospitals for the care of the "inebriate" were erected. After the turn of the 20th century, the idea of a disease was actually lost a bit in the furor over prohibition. A few physicians still treated the illness, and some of them were helpful to the founders of Alcoholics Anonymous. In 1937, a group called the Research Council on Problems of Alcohol was founded that proposed research on alcoholism as a disease comparable to "tuberculosis, poliomyelitis, cancer, and other major diseases." In 1956, the American Medical Association (AMA) established a committee on alcoholism and stated that alcoholism is "an illness which should have the attention of a physician."

---

[2] William L. White. Slaying the Dragon: The History of Addiction Treatment and Recovery in America, (1998) Chestnut Health Systems / Lighthouse Institute, ISBN 0-938475-07-X.

So you can see that the idea of addiction as a disease is not a new one. Even as medical professionals learned in school that addiction is a treatable disease, many didn't believe it. They couldn't see it under the microscope or dissect it in anatomy lab. If there isn't a test for it, it doesn't exist. So for many doctors the time of realization is still happening.

4. What is addiction?

Addiction is a primary, brain based, largely genetic, behavioral illness that is chronic, progressive, incurable, and, in most cases, terminal. There are a lot of words in that sentence and most need some explaining.

"Primary": This means that it's an illness in itself. Most psychiatrists used to think that addiction was a manifestation of other illnesses or personality traits. If you had addiction you needed treatment for depression, anxiety or a personality disorder. In the last 15 years it has become clear that addiction has its own biology and natural history. You don't need to have any other diagnosis to explain addiction. Also you don't have to abuse drugs to create addiction. It can exist on its own.

"Brain based": This means that the biology of addiction is in the brain. While that might seem simple and easy to understand, it's really quite a new idea. Addiction is a brain disorder, but the symptoms often seem to control or come from other areas of the body. But an alcoholic's problem isn't in his liver. An obese compulsive overeater doesn't have a stomach problem. Consequently, before we knew about the biology of addiction, we used to focus on those areas in treatment. That gave us the idea that we can cure addiction in a compulsive overeater by stapling his stomach or treat an alcoholic with a medicine that makes him sick if he drinks.

"Largely genetic": There's an idea in science called variance. It means how much of an outcome is explained by a particular situation. So with addiction we would ask what amount of variance is explained by genetics. It turns out to be a pretty high number. Something on the order of 70% of the variance of who becomes an addict is explained by their genetic makeup. There are other factors as well.

"Chronic": Most of American Medicine is focused on acute illnesses; those are illnesses that go away. Someone is well, then they get sick, then they get well again. That's acute. Chronic is different. Chronic illness lingers; not all are incurable, but most are. Think of diabetes. You don't cure it; you control it and learn to live with it. It's the same with addiction. It's not going away. The person doesn't grow out of it, nor does it burn out. The solution isn't to wait until it goes away. The solution is to learn a way to live with it. Some people reading this may be confused at this point. They may be thinking, "How can you have addiction if you don't use drugs?" Addiction the disease doesn't go away when the addiction behavior stops; the symptoms are still there. The symptoms are what lead to relapse of the addiction behavior unless the addicted person finds another way to live that keeps the symptoms in check.

"Progressive": This means that addicts get worse over time, not better. Progressive doesn't mean there's no hope, and it doesn't mean the addict has to use. What becomes worse are the untreated symptoms of the illness. Without treatment and recovery things don't go well, but we have treatment and recovery that provides an excellent prognosis and can provide a daily arrest of the symptoms.

"Incurable": There is no cure for addiction--no shot or medicine that will make it go away. Again, like diabetes, we don't aim for a cure but for a way to live with the presence of the disease without letting the disease ruin the patient's life. In diabetes our goal is to return blood sugar levels to normal so that the extra sugar doesn't damage the patient's health. In addiction we seek a remission of the symptoms so that the person with addiction does not seek out drugs or other behaviors to fix the symptoms himself.

"Terminal": In most cases the end result of addiction, if left untreated, is death, again like diabetes. In the end there are many ways to die of addiction: suicide, poisoning, overdose, homicide, trauma, and many others. But in the final analysis it is the illness of addiction that leads to death. Even if the people with addiction manage to never use their drug or behavior of choice again, without treatment the symptoms of the disease will worsen and they will eventually not want to go on living.

So putting all that together, what is addiction? It's just one more serious illness that we as a society have to learn to live with.

It's not drug use. If it were the solution would be easy; tie addicts to the bed and they don't use drugs. If you do that you haven't solved anything. What you have is the untreated disease of addiction and a miserable person who doesn't feel good and can't function. Like every other human being on the planet, they want to feel normal. Their brains remember what made them feel normal, and they'll be going to get it as soon as you let them up; unless, of course, another solution is available.

5. If drug use isn't a symptom of addiction, what are the symptoms?

Our society likes to think that drugs cause addiction. It's actually the other way around for most people with addiction. The addiction causes the drug use. To explain this better I'll have to tell you some of the anatomy of the brain that involves addiction. The picture below is a crude diagram of a part of the brain called the reward center.

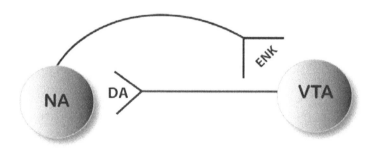

The circle labeled VTA represents a group of brain cells (neurons) called the Ventral Tegmental Area. They produce a neurotransmitter called dopamine (DA), which they release to provide a signal to other neurons. They send this dopamine signal to another group of cells called the Nucleus Accumbens (NA). This is where the magic happens. Whatever you're doing when a big slug of dopamine hits the shell of the Nucleus Accumbens gets coded as a good thing that's necessary for survival and that you should do more of. Dopamine at the Nucleus Accumbens is why we do anything twice. For normal people normal levels of dopamine release provide normal levels of pleasure and reward. But some people don't have normal levels of dopamine and so normal activities don't lead to normal reward. They need bigger stimulation to feel what other people feel normally.

This idea of dopamine level is best expressed as something called "dopamine tone." In its role as a signal, the dopamine goes from the VTA into the space between its neuron and the Nucleus Accumbens. On the surface of the NA are receptors that "see" the dopamine. The amount of dopamine released, the number of receptors, and the time the dopamine is out there touching the receptors go together to make up the dopamine tone. We'll talk more about that later.

Notice that the Nucleus Accumbens is not only important to life and happiness, but it's also very polite. It sends a thank you card back to the VTA in the form of another neurotransmitter called enkephalin, the brain's own opiates. This provides a positive feedback loop. The more dopamine released, the more enkephalin released; the more enkephalin released, the more dopamine is released. If this loop continues, it goes on until all the dopamine that was lined up on the edge of the cell is gone, and the level of dopamine falls very rapidly. In fact it falls so rapidly that the person ends up feeling worse than he did before he used. Of course he's going to want to find more of what he used to get his level back up. Anybody would.

Another thing the Nucleus Accumbens does is send a signal using a different neurotransmitter, called serotonin, to a part of the brain called the frontal cortex. That signal is felt as self-esteem or "I'm doing okay." If you don't have enough dopamine function, you don't get that signal.

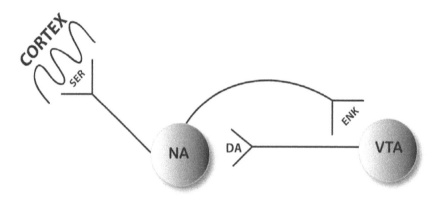

So let's imagine what it would be like without enough dopamine in the system. Little things would not excite us or matter to us. We would have difficulty paying attention and remembering things because those actions require dopamine. Normal pleasures would give us nothing at all, and we'd look around at other people enjoying themselves and wonder what is wrong with us. We'd feel alone and pretty much less than others. Because nothing much was rewarding, there would not be much reason to get up off the sofa. If we were born this way, we'd have no way to identify it as an illness because we've never known anything else. Just as sight for someone born blind would just be something other people could do, so would enjoying little things be for us. Until of course we found a drug that raised our dopamine and made us feel pretty good. With the higher dopamine level we could feel comfortable and relaxed. We could enjoy little things; we could feel a part of the world. It would be like a congenitally blind person suddenly able to see. What percentage of them do you think would be satisfied with their new found sight going away after a few minutes and then being told they could never have it again? Well, that's about the percentage of addicts who would be satisfied to just stop using and go back to the way they've felt all their lives.

Addiction isn't using drugs; it's what it feels like to the addict to live without using drugs. The symptoms are what people with addiction feel when they aren't using, not what happens when they do.

6. So what happens when we take a drug?

You would probably think that the answer is something that has only recently been discovered but that's not so. In 1988, two Italian researchers[3] published a paper that showed exactly what happened to dopamine levels in the brain after the administration of drugs. They were able to do this with a pretty ingenious method of real time measurement of the dopamine release at the Nucleus Accumbens. What they found was that regardless of drug class (sedative, narcotic, stimulant, or nicotine) they all released dopamine at the Nucleus Accumbens. The behavioral effects of the drug could be blocked by blocking the dopamine receptor. The dopamine blocker also blocked the behavioral response to food.

In addition to blocking the effects by blocking dopamine receptors, the drugs' effects could be blocked by various other means, according to the drug being affected. For instance, opioid blockers blocked the effect of morphine and methadone, while nicotine receptor blockers blocked the effect of nicotine. So it's been a while now that we've known, or should have known, that while drugs work via different receptors and different methods to make the reward system activated, they all produce the same final

---

[3] Di Chiara G and Imperato A. Drugs Abused by Humans Preferentially Increase Synaptic Dopamine Concentrations in the Mesolimbic System of Freely Moving Rats. Proceedings of the National Academy of Sciences of the US of A 1988;85: 5274-5278.

common effect, reward system activation. While it took scientists a long time to figure that out, it seems pretty much like common sense when you think about it. If it doesn't activate the reward system, why use it twice?

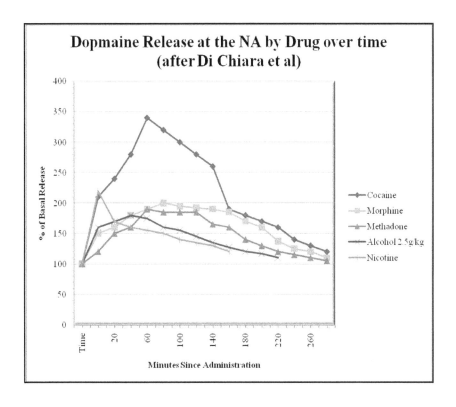

As you can see by the chart, the drugs work at different time intervals, and it looks like everything returns to normal after the drugs wear off. But we have to remember the dopamine level isn't the whole story. What counts is the dopamine tone, which is a combination of how much dopamine is there for how long and also how many receptors we have to see the dopamine.

As the dopamine level spikes, the receptors go away in order to protect the system from too much dopamine. The more dopamine released, the more receptors will go away. So while the amount of dopamine at 100 minutes after taking a drug might look like it's higher than normal, the person will actually feel worse than when he started because there are fewer dopamine receptors and less dopamine signal will get through. So instead of being a peak and a slow return to normal, it really feels something like this:

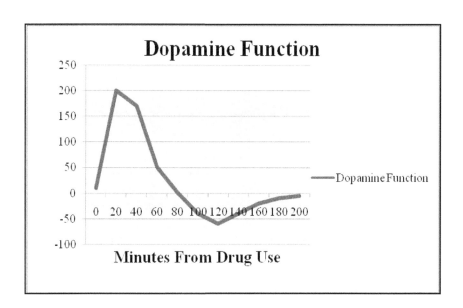

7. **Can too much dopamine protect you from addiction?**

Before I answer that, I'm going to have to draw you another picture:

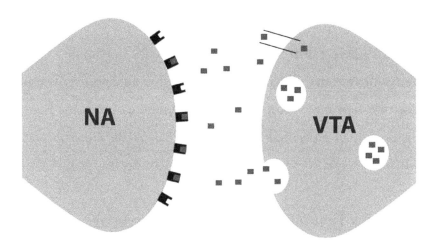

This is a close up picture of where the arm of the dopamine-producing VTA neuron comes up close to the body of a NA neuron. The neuron on the right is the VTA neuron and the little squares are dopamine molecules. Some are being packaged for release and some are being released right now. The straight tube near the top of the neuron is something new you haven't heard about here yet, a dopamine transporter. The dopamine transporter is like a vacuum cleaner that sucks up all the extra dopamine so it can be recycled. The neuron on the left is the NA neuron. Those figures on it are the dopamine receptors. So the dopamine is released by the VTA, stays in the area between the cell (the synapse), and acts on the dopamine receptors. This picture lets us make up a kind of equation for dopamine tone or dopamine signal:

DA tone = DA molecules X DA receptors X TIME

Where TIME is the amount of time the dopamine molecules are in the synapse. The dopamine transporters determine the time. The more receptors and the better they work, the less time the dopamine stays out to produce a signal. So the equation can be written:

$$\textbf{DA Tone} = \frac{\textbf{DA molecules X DA Receptors}}{\textbf{DA transporters}}$$

Now that you know what determines the dopamine tone let's take a look at how dopamine tone can protect someone from addiction. In a recent study at Brookhaven National Laboratory, researchers looked at non-alcoholics with at least three first-degree alcoholic relatives. You would expect such a person to have a high risk of alcoholism and the question is, "Why aren't they alcoholic?" Well, it turns out that they have a higher than normal level of dopamine receptors and can feel positive rewards better than most people.[4] Here's a group that you'd expect, from family history, to not be able to feel reward and to crave alcohol. But they are different not only from their family but from most people because they have more dopamine receptors than normal, a very protective trait. They feel naturally what people with addiction wants to feel and can feel a bit when they are using.

But there are also people who have way too much dopamine function, and they have problems too. Too much dopamine function usually makes you anxious and not in the normal way. Too much dopamine makes you so focused that everything seems important and you become compulsive and obsessive. Many such people have repetitive panic attacks or Obsessive-Compulsive Disorder, a serious mental illness that can destroy people's lives. Such people sometimes look for sedatives to make them feel better (they don't like cocaine or stimulants as they make them feel worse). They can, through the use of sedatives, damage the VTA enough to become addicted.

This is a very important point that can get lost in learning about the neurobiology of addiction. While most people, I believe, have addiction because of an inborn or genetic problem, some can have it develop because of the use of a drug. But remember that this is the path of the minority of people with addiction. So the

---

[4] Volkow ND, et al. High Levels of Dopamine D2 Receptors in Unaffected Members of Alcoholic Families: Possible Protective Factors. Arch Gen Psychiatry 2006 Sep; 63(9):999-1008.

thing that is protective isn't too much dopamine but the right amount of dopamine; too much can be a problem for developing addiction as well.

8. What's an addicting drug?

We have to make a distinction here: the difference between a drug that can cause addiction and one that an addict will want to use. I make that distinction because I think that most people with addiction didn't need to have it caused. They had the biology and then found a drug that made them feel normal. That's very different than the drug causing the problem.

So a drug or behavior that an addict will use to feel better is anything that raises their dopamine high enough to be close to normal. The brain doesn't actually care if it's heroin in the vein or a box of chocolate cookies. All it sees is the dopamine. The drug will have to work fast enough to become associated with the dopamine rise or it won't get used again, and it will have to raise the dopamine up sufficiently to have an effect. Not all drugs or behaviors will do this for all people, so you find some who like one drug or behavior while some others use a different one to treat their symptoms.

So what is a drug that can cause addiction? That would be one, like those mentioned above, that raise dopamine fast enough and high enough to be of use to the addicted individual but also so high that it's too much of a signal. In that event the brain has to compensate by decreasing the number of dopamine receptors or maybe some of the VTA cells will die, sort of like a fuse has to blow when lightning hits your house. With the loss of dopamine signal, the problem gets worse. I can imagine someone who is not addicted and who uses for another reason (peer pressure, for instance) who causes damage with each use. Eventually the dopamine level is low enough that he needs to use to feel normal. Again, I must emphasize that this scenario only accounts for about 20% of the addicts I meet. Most addicts can clearly remember symptoms of addiction their entire lives.

9. If the reward system is the problem, can't we just remove it?

That's a surprisingly common question. People with the disease of addiction can be so desperate for relief that they'd be willing to have brain surgery to cut the reward center out of their skull if it would stop their using. Unfortunately, that really wouldn't help.

The Medial Forebrain Bundle (MFB), where the reward system is located, is a very deep brain structure. It's very old and set in its ways, and it needs to be because it handles our survival decisions. When you are in a starvation situation and have to decide whether or not you should steal some food, it handles that decision without you having to think about it. The MFB also handles it in a way that would make it unlikely for you to override the decision even if you didn't want to steal the food. Survival mechanisms have to be that way; they have to be unconscious, automatic, and hard or impossible to override. Otherwise they wouldn't work.

If our ancestors didn't have the MFB telling them what to do to stay alive, I would never have written this and you wouldn't be reading it. Neither one of us would be here. If we get rid of the MFB now so that addicts will stop using, then we can kiss our great grandchildren goodbye. You can't get rid of a species survival mechanism and expect that species to survive. We also have to understand that if some system exists in the body, there will be some people who have something wrong with that system. That's really all addiction is, something wrong with the reward system. We would never advocate getting rid of lungs to stop tuberculosis. So why consider getting rid of the MFB to stop addiction?

10. Can't we just block the dopamine?

Nice try. Sorry, that still wouldn't work and anyone with addiction would be able to tell you why. If you just block a drug's ability to work but leave the disease untreated, the disease will find another way to get what it needs. Besides, doctors have already tried it and it didn't work. Rather than decrease the effectiveness of gambling to make someone high, a dopamine blocker actually made the subjects gamble even more.[5] This finding has the scientists confused, but anyone with addiction can tell you why. The medicine caused the baseline level of dopamine down even further, so they needed more gambling to get relief.

At first, and still to some extent, doctors thought a drug that blocked the enkephalin receptor would do the trick. And to a large extent it does, if the idea is to stop drug use. With the enkephalin blocker onboard, the compulsive use cycle doesn't spike up as high or as fast so that some drugs don't give enough reward to be useful. So people will generally stop using them. But remember, drug use is not the same as addiction. What we do in many cases is take someone who can use a drug and feel normal for a little while and make it impossible to make him feel normal at all.

---

[5] Goudriaan AE; et al. Decision Making in Pathological Gambling: A Comparison Between Pathological Gamblers, Alcohol Dependents, Persons with Tourette's Syndrome, and Normal Controls. *Cognitive Brain Research* 23(1): 137-151, 2005.

A recent study shows that even when the enkephalin blocker works, it only works for people with a specific mutation of their enkephalin receptor. So there are some people who may have that specific mutation and not have a low dopamine that will benefit from such a blocker. But while they have compulsive drug use, it isn't clear to me that when the dust settles we'll still say that what's wrong with these people is addiction.

11. Can you be addicted to something good?

As soon as we start talking about good and bad we've left medicine and science and entered the world of moral judgments. I just don't have any data on moral judgments, so you'll have to decide for yourself what's good and bad. Now if what you mean by "good" is "good for you," I may have something to say.

Many people ask me if it's okay to switch to being addicted to exercise because it's so good for them. Well, moderate exercise is good for you; compulsive over-doing it isn't. Just as you might have heard that a drink a day is heart healthy, but heavy drinking isn't good for you. So I'd like you to let go of the idea that the drug or behavior is good or bad. It's not the drug or behavior but rather the way it is used that determines the harmful consequences. In that light anything used to feed the disease of addiction won't be good for you in the long run.

Several of my patients told me they were able to stop using the drug that was troublesome only to gain 70 pounds or lose thousands at the casino. That doesn't do anyone any good. The key is to treat the underlying illness not just switch to something you think is a safe drug. In addiction, no drug stays safe for long.

12. Can we just get rid of the drug?

That's a pretty common idea and a pretty common solution to attempt. Our culture tried that with alcohol back in the 20's. The argument is that alcohol prohibition decreased drinking and decreased alcoholism even after prohibition ended. Here's a chart of gallons of alcohol consumed by every 10 people. It shows that, indeed, prohibition (the area of missing data) decreased drinking behavior. Before prohibition on average every 10 people drank 20 gallons a year; after prohibition every 10 people only drank 10 gallons a year.

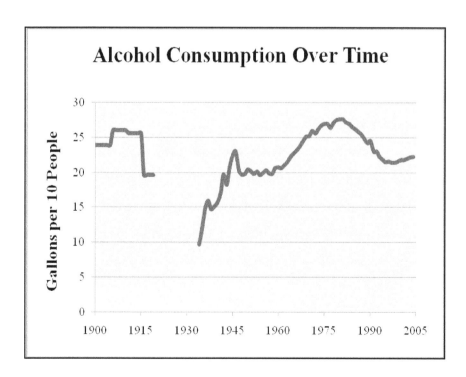

But what happened to the alcoholics? Did they disappear? Did they stop drinking? Did they use something else? What other common drugs might they have switched to now that they couldn't get alcohol? Here's a graph of cigarette use per person. This graph is in 100's of cigarettes so that in 1920 the average American was smoking about 600-700 a year. By 1934 the average was over 1000. There's no blank on this graph because there was no prohibition of cigarettes and we have data for every year.

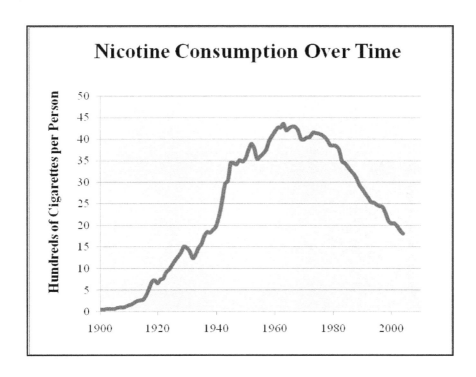

But what if we got the same thing from alcohol as cigarettes? What if the disease of addiction is a brain disease that doesn't particularly care what drug we use? What would be the effect of alcohol prohibition then? In science when you want to see if two variables interact, one simple way to do that is to multiply them. Since people drink to get dopamine and they smoke to get dopamine, we can see the effect of alcohol prohibition on this made up "Dopamine Load" which is the combined use of cigarettes and alcohol.

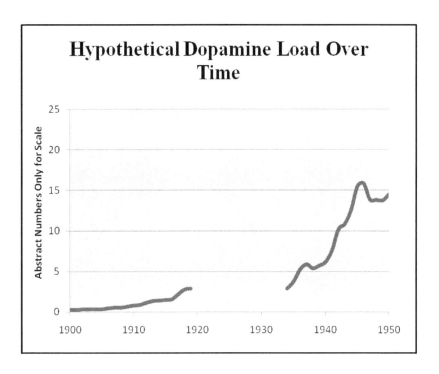

Questions and Answers on Addiction

I made the preceding graph a close up so you can see that making alcohol illegal didn't change the combined use of cigarettes and alcohol at all. Just as much of the combination was used after prohibition as before. But you may also notice that the combined use rises a good bit after prohibition. We need to know that there is good evidence that dopamine receptor levels decrease with certain stresses. Remember the equation I showed you; lower dopamine receptors mean lower dopamine signal. Take a look at the next graph in relation to the great depression and World Wars. Notice the drop off at the end of WWII and the blip during Korea, then the rise during the social upheavals of Vietnam and the inflationary spiral of the 70's.

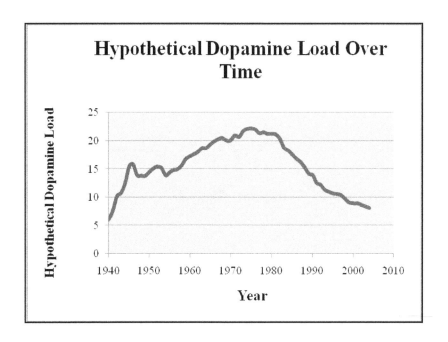

But did life get a lot easier in America in the 1980's? We worked on nicotine suppression, and we continued to tell people how dangerous alcohol is. So if they stopped using these drugs as much, did they just need less dopamine? Was Ronald Regan that good a president that no one needed extra dopamine anymore? Or did they switch to something else?

The USDA keeps track of the calories that are taken in per capita every year. Before the 1950's the data is erratic due to the depression and the rationing during the wars. But you can see that when we got the message about alcohol and cigarettes around 1980, we just went out and found a new reward—excess food.

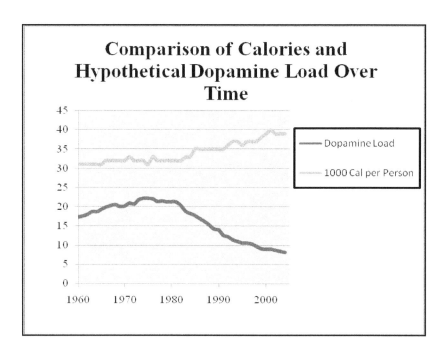

So what generally happens when we get rid of a drug is that people with addiction are not going to relax and say "Oh well, I guess I'll just not use it anymore." They go find another drug.

13. Why does addiction get worse?

Addiction is a progressive disease. That means it gets worse with time whether the person with addiction is using something or not. The reason is that we lose dopamine producing cells as we age. This was shown by Dr. Nora Volkow at her lab in Brookhaven, New York.[6] Averaged over her subjects, Dr. Volkow found that we lose about 7% of our dopamine receptors with every decade of life. She also looked at the decrease in dopamine producing neurons in the reward system and found that they may decrease with age as well. Sort of a double whammy, isn't it? Well there's actually a triple whammy. Along with the dopamine receptor decrease in the reward center, we get a serotonin receptor decrease in the frontal cortex.[7] That's important because the Nucleus Accumbens sends a serotonin signal to the frontal cortex that lets us know we're a good person. Many have noticed that low self-esteem is a natural part of addiction, and I think this is one reason for it. If the MFB isn't functioning right, we aren't getting enough serotonin to our frontal cortex.

---

[6] ND Volkow, et al. Dopamine Transporters Decrease with Age. Journal of Nuclear Medicine, Vol 37, Issue 4 1996: 554-559.

[7] Wang GJ, et al. Evaluation of Age-related Changes in Serotonin 5-HT2 and Dopamine D2 Receptor Availability in Healthy Human Subjects. Life Sci. 1995;56(14):PL249-53.

So basically with age we make less dopamine, can use less of the dopamine that we make, and can't send the signal from the reward center to the frontal cortex as well either. You're probably thinking this is hopeless, aren't you?

I don't think it is. We know we can raise dopamine receptor levels by changing behavior and thinking (as in recovery), and we can raise levels of dopamine and serotonin with medications. So while we can't stop aging, we can treat the effects.

14. So is this why an addict uses more over time?

In part that's true, but most people find that their drug use escalates much faster than 7% a decade. Most people attribute the increased need for their substance or behavior to tolerance, or what science calls neuro-adaptation. Before I tell you why I think addicts use more over time, I have to tell you a bit about tolerance.

Tolerance, neuro-adaptation, is when a nerve adjusts to a stimulating signal in order to go back to the way it was before it got the signal. For instance, let's say that a guy who's never had any alcohol takes a drink. Immediately, in order to keep him from falling over, his brain cells change the receptor that sees the alcohol. They've gotten too big a signal, and if the brain decreases the number of receptors that see alcohol, the signal will go down. Some tolerance is fast like that and some is slower, requiring about two weeks or so. Alcohol is the classic drug when you look at tolerance; the more you drink the more you are used to it, the more tolerant you are. So you can explain why an alcoholic who started drinking a six pack a day is 4 years later drinking a case a day and still feeling the same level of "drunk." But what about a drug like cocaine? It doesn't cause tolerance; it causes something like the opposite called sensitization. Why do cocaine users need more cocaine after using for a while if it causes the opposite of tolerance?

Now we come to what I think is the real reason we use more drug after a while. If it was tolerance, cocaine users would pick a dose and stick with it, but that doesn't happen. The real reason I think we need more and more drug as time goes by (or more and more food, sex, gambling, just fill in the blank) is because of how the Nucleus Accumbens works. Remember I told you about the dopamine level in the Medial Forebrain Bundle and how the dopamine hits the Nucleus Accumbens? We called it the reward signal. What it more specifically and accurately encodes is not just reward but something called "Reward Prediction Error." In a study at Columbia[8], researchers found that this area of the brain compares the current reward with the average reward and only fires when the current reward is greater than the expected average of what had come before.

So there's an anticipatory rush when someone gets access to a drug that made them feel good before. Then they use the drug. The Midbrain Dopamine cells calculate the difference between the reward they're getting now and what they had gotten from prior experiences with the drug. If it isn't better, there's not as much signal. Did you ever try to recapture a particular event that was really good? You did everything the same and still it wasn't the same. That's because the signal you got the first time was partly

---

[8] Bayer HM and Glimcher PW. Midbrain Dopamine Neurons Encode a Quantitative Reward Prediction Error Signal. Neuron 47, 2005: 129-141.

the surprise of a better than expected reward. The second time there was no extra punch because the reward wasn't better than the average of what had come before. So that's one of the reasons I think people use more and more drug over time regardless of whether the drug causes tolerance or not; the only way to boost the signal is to increase the unexpectedness of the stimulus.

15. Did I cause this?

What an excellent question. For most of the people reading this book I'd say the answer is "no." I believe that most people with addiction are born with the biology for the disease, and it is that biology that leads to the drug use and not the other way around. Why I believe that is a long explanation and is covered in the questions to follow.

16. What are Type I and Type II addiction?

Back in 1987 a researcher named Cloninger proposed a classification of two types of alcoholism[9]. With great imagination, he named them as Type I and Type II. Anyway, he said that Type I represented the majority of alcoholics and that it was characterized by four things:

1.   late onset (after age 25)
2.   low degree of spontaneous alcohol seeking
3.   psychological dependence coupled with guilt and fear
4.   and a low degree of novelty seeking and a high degree of harm avoidance.

That was a pretty astute observation, and, of course, Type II alcoholism was just the reverse: early onset, novelty seeking, and a lot of spontaneous alcohol seeking and not much guilt or fear. What Cloninger didn't know about back in 1987 was the dopamine reward system of the Medial Forebrain Bundle. If you take a look at these types through the dopamine system, what you see is what you would expect to see from people who had too

---

[9] Cloninger CR: Neurogenetic Adaptive Mechanisms in Alcoholism. Science 236: 410-416, 1987.

much dopamine (type I) and too little dopamine (type II). To understand these types better we have to leave humans for a bit and head off with some rat researchers.

It turns out that rats, regular rats that is, don't really like drinking alcohol. It burns. So to get a rat in a lab to drink alcohol you have to do what the liquor industry did for my generation; you have to make a wine cooler. You add sugar to the alcohol, and the rats liking for sugar overcomes its dislike for alcohol and it eventually will drink the stuff.

So you start by adding a little sugar and a few of the rats will drink it. As you add more and more sugar, more and more rats will start drinking. Eventually you'll add enough sugar so that only the very few rats that are most averse to alcohol will not have started drinking. If you line these rats up in the order they started drinking you get the scientific bell shaped curve (see below). Now you take the rats on the right of the curve (they like alcohol the least) and mate the males and females together. You do the same for the rats on the left of the curve (they dislike alcohol the least). Now you have two new sets of rats --those descended from the left hand of the curve and those descended from the right hand side of the curve. With each of those two groups you do the same experiment, each time taking the extreme right or left and mating them together to make yet another group. So in each generation you get a bell shaped curve, but the curves get farther and farther apart. After about 14 or 15 generations you now have two new strains of rats.

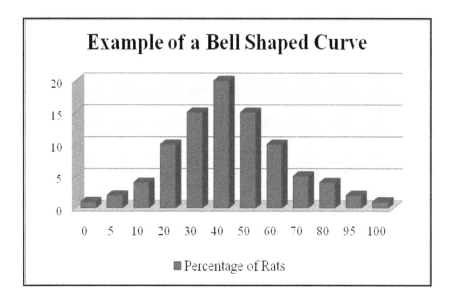

Those rats descended from the right hand side of the curve don't like alcohol at all. They won't self administer drugs. They just don't see the point. The rats descended from the left hand side of the curve are very different. They'll drink straight lab alcohol with no sugar. They love self administering drugs.

The first group is the Fisher rats and the second group is the Lewis rats.[10] When you take a look at the brains of the Lewis rats what you see is a dopamine system that isn't healthy. There's not

---

[10] Flores G, Wood GK, et al. Lewis and Fischer rats: A Comparison of Dopamine Transporter and Receptor Levels. Brain Research 1998 Dec 14: 814(1-2):34-40.

enough dopamine signal to feel normal, and they are looking for every source of dopamine they can find. Think of these as Type II's. On the other hand, the Fisher rats have more dopamine receptors than normal, so any extra dopamine actually makes them feel bad. They don't like it and won't use it. Think of them as Type I's for a while.

Now I said that the Fisher rats won't use drugs and that's true, but you can change that if you want. Let's say you force the drugs on them by putting in a catheter and pumping them full of, say, heroin or cocaine, the way the Lewis rat would take it. Every time they get the hit, some damage is done to the dopamine system because the drug is just "too much." Remember the fuse that blows to protect the house from lightning? So after a while they have less and less dopamine until, at some point, they no longer act like Fisher rats but start acting like Lewis rats.

Now it's time to realize that this experiment was first done by nature and we were the subjects. Some of us were born as Lewis rats and some as Fisher rats, but most of us were born in the middle. For the "Lewis" people, I pretty much think the die was cast. They were going to find the dopamine no matter where they had to look.

For most of the "Fisher" people, everything might have been okay except that too much dopamine actually makes us nervous and we seek relief from the anxiety. Alcohol and downers are good for that, and Type I's tend to prefer those. Of course every time a Type I person drinks or uses downers, there's that same boost of dopamine in the reward center even though there's too much dopamine in the "anxiety centers" of the brain. After a while they have too little dopamine in the reward centers and start to look for alcohol and drugs even without the anxiety.

My clinical experience is different from Cloninger's. Most, about 80%, of the people I talk to with addiction are Type II's. Type I's are not that common in my practice. Back in the 80's people thought alcoholism and drug addiction were two different things, so when they studied alcoholics, they tried to get a pure population. They excluded those alcoholics who used other drugs. If you do that you will get a population over-represented by Type I's, and I think that's what happened with Cloninger's research.

17. Can you get addiction even if you aren't born with it?

Yes, I think you can. Let's say that you are not born with the genetic types listed previously. Let's say you're born "normal." When everyone else is experimenting with drugs, you try it and it may be somewhat enjoyable but not really all that much. There may be consequences or not, but let's say there were some and you decide you really don't think it's worth it to keep using the drug. But you do think it's important to keep your friends and they think it's important to keep using the drug. So you put up with it. Remember the damage that's done to the reward system when too much dopamine is released at one time. As that damage progresses you become lower and lower in your dopamine tone. It's quite possible that eventually you can bring your brain to the level where you need the drug to feel normal.

Now this is society's vision of how *everyone* gets addicted. In my experience very few people follow this path to addiction.

There is another, more common way to become addicted if you weren't born that way. Of course how we get addicted doesn't differ much for the person with the problem. There are certain stressors, especially certain social stressors that can lower the density of dopamine receptors on the cells of the Nucleus Accumbens. Remember that with fewer dopamine receptors we get a lower dopamine tone and a lower ability to feel reward. So someone born "normal" who is subjected to these social stresses may experience life the way someone would who was born with a dopamine receptors that didn't work right. More on this later, but if you're wondering what these stresses are, they are being alone and feeling less than others.

18. Where is addiction in the brain?

Well, it kind of depends on what you mean by addiction. I'll give you the whole thing and let you figure out what part you are interested in.

Earlier we discussed the reward center of the brain, and I showed you the dopamine-enkephalin feedback loop. That's the biology of the compulsive use part of addiction. Before we go on to another part though, there's something I want to add.

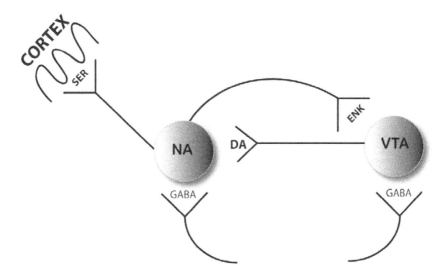

As you can see in the diagram both the NA and the VTA have inputs that use a neurotransmitter called GABA. Specifically they both have on their surfaces a special type of GABA receptor

47

called GABA receptor b (GABAb). When the GABAb receptor is stimulated, it is more difficult for that cell to fire and send a signal. Think of it as a kind of dimmer switch. Energy is still going through, just not as much. So the cycle doesn't go so far out of control. This may not seem relevant right now but it will be later when we talk about treatment.

Well that's it for compulsive use. What about withdrawal? Withdrawal doesn't happen in the same place, and I'll tell you how I know that. If you insert a small micro catheter into the Medial Forebrain Bundle (MFB) of a mammal and hook it up to a drug, let's say heroin, the animal will be happy to self inject the drug all the time. Now he's only getting a little bit; so little, in fact, that it's only going to the MFB. The rest of the brain can't see it. So let's say you let him self inject a few hours every day for weeks and weeks. Now stop the heroin. What happens? No withdrawal. So the MFB handles compulsive use but not withdrawal.

Quite a long ways away (a few inches is a very long way when you're the size of a brain cell) is another part of the brain called the Periaqueductal Gray (PG). If you put a micro catheter in the PG, an animal won't self administer drug a there. Even a Lewis rat won't self administer a drug to the PG. No one would, because there's no reward. So obviously the PG doesn't have anything to do with compulsive use. However if you inject the drug, let's say heroin, every day into the animal's PG, then the PG can get exposed to the drug as if the animal was compulsively using. Now after several weeks you stop doing it. The animal goes into withdrawal. So the PG is no compulsive use, but a lot of withdrawal and the MFB is no withdrawal, but a lot of compulsive use.

Well, we covered compulsive use and withdrawal. What else is there? Relapse.

Before I tell you about the relapse circuit, I should mention that there are relapses associated with both of the areas we talked about already. Obviously if someone is in withdrawal they will use to prevent withdrawal, and if they are walking around with a low dopamine in the MFB, restless, irritable, and discontented, they are prone to relapse just to feel better. But I want to describe a different kind of relapse, the "out-of-the-blue" relapse.

The out-of-the-blue relapse comes from a signal using a neurotransmitter called glutamate. The glutamate is sent to the MFB from the area of the brain that remembers emotions. It's what people have experienced as "euphoric recall," and it's a very powerful trigger. Imagine an alcoholic has been sober for a good while, and then he goes to a wedding. Everybody's drinking, he gets euphoric recall and, even though he went to the wedding intending not to drink, he orders a drink. It's important to know that this kind of relapse is real because there are medicines used to block this type of trigger by modulating down the glutamate signal.

In summary, there are three parts of the brain in addiction: compulsive use, withdrawal, and relapse. They need to be taken into account separately and at different time intervals in deciding what medication would be of help.

19. What is Harm Reduction?

Sorry, this is a complicated answer, so you may need to read this part a couple of times. One of the problems is that my definition of harm reduction seems to be the exact opposite of most other people's definition. I think you'll like mine better, but first I'll explain the other, more popular definition.

Harm reduction is basically any treatment aimed at reducing harm in the addict's life short of stopping the drug and achieving abstinence. An example would be considered such things as a clean-needle programs, though I know some addiction medicine doctors who would call methadone, a treatment for addiction, a harm reduction because the person is still taking "a drug." In this view treatment is not aided by medication and harm reduction is used to refer to interventions for the person who won't stop. For most people who practice addiction medicine, this idea of harm reduction is looked at as a lower form of treatment, or a sort of secondary fall back position.

On the other hand I look at it backwards. I see the idea of abstinence as harm reduction. For me the disease is present whether the person is using or not. Using is not the important issue, and stopping isn't the goal of treatment. Resolution of the original symptoms is the goal, and just achieving abstinence won't get you there. As I said before, what you get when you make someone stop using is a miserable addict. So this emphasis on stopping the drug use looks like harm reduction to me. It isn't treatment of the illness, but it does get rid of some of the harm the drug might cause (liver disease, etc).

Now for those of you who are jumping up and down right now swearing that I'll roast in hell for such heresy let me remind you that I don't advocate using drugs. I believe that the human brain with addiction can not choose what chemicals it needs when it thinks it needs it. I'm turning this "harm reduction" phrase on its head to make a point. The abstinence based "crowd" largely looks down its nose at the harm reduction folks. I'd just like them to see it from another angle.

In the end we all want the same things. We want people with addiction to be happy, joyous, and free. We want people to feel normal and engage in normal life without having to use short acting drugs that cause crashes and worsening of the illness. We all want the illness treated. I think we, as a professional field, just need a different idea about what that treatment entails.

20. Any harm in looking at addiction a different way?

There is one main proposition held by most other physicians that I cannot accept. It is that the using of a drug is the main symptom of addiction and, consequently, that the goal is to stop drug use. This idea leads to a number of erroneous conclusions. First, that the use of different drugs or behaviors represents different diseases. Also coming from this common assumption is the idea that once the use stops for a prolonged period, the illness will be in remission. I've had many arguments with colleagues over this idea, and what amazes me most is not that they think these are the best conclusions to be drawn from the evidence, but that they think these are the conclusions they must follow because my own are not politically popular. They express a fear that if my conclusions were generally accepted, society would decrease its support for addiction medicine within the larger body of medicine. I was greatly surprised to find this out. I had assumed that the issue was one of facts and data. I was prepared to argue my point and was flabbergasted to hear answers such as, "yes but..."

"...if we say that, no one will ever accept addiction medicine as a specialty because there are no specialties based on a single disease."

"...if I tell Congress these are all the same thing, you can forget them taking heroin addiction seriously."

"… if we say that, then no one will ever come to our treatment program because no one will be willing to give up all their drugs at once."

"...can you imagine what the insurance companies will say if we're treating for addiction and we list 'debting' as the drug of choice?"

"...that would change everything."

I sometimes get tired and want to give up. It would be a lot easier to just agree with everyone. But think of what happens when you make medical decisions based on politics rather than data. Can you imagine the outcome? Is there a line outside your senator's office of people looking for medical advice? And people don't make appointments with me to hear my political views either. I meet a lot of people who have been hurt by this political compromise. Many of them have stories of relatives who died of this disease because they got treatment based on what I believe are false premises. I have known some people who died when they might have lived if their doctors knew better.

Here's an example of what I mean. A man I treated had been drinking for over 20 years. Before seeing me he saw a psychiatrist who believed the drinking was the disease. With some help, the man stopped drinking. After the initial euphoria of freedom wore off, he started to feel the real symptoms of the disease. As he couldn't drink anymore, he had no way to feel better. His psychiatrist felt that since the man's "new" symptoms weren't caused by his drinking, they must represent "Major Depression," and he started him on an anti-depressant that raises the serotonin level in the brain. As a boost of serotonin gives us a feeling of wellbeing, the patient responded and the psychiatrist felt he had made a good decision. As weeks went by the man noticed an almost imperceptible gradual worsening. He didn't enjoy things as much, couldn't think as clearly, couldn't remember as well, and started to eat more junk food and gain weight. Eventually he lost his interest in almost everything and was having cravings to drink again. His doctor felt this must represent breakthrough depression and raised the dose of the anti-depressant. It worked for a few weeks and then the man was feeling worse than ever.

What neither the doctor nor the patient knew is that high serotonin levels decrease the release of dopamine in the reward center[11]. The man never had Major Depression; he was experiencing the unmasked symptoms of the disease of addiction. Giving the right treatment for depression eventually made the patient worse. As he didn't drink again, the psychiatrist didn't recognize worsening addiction. As the man eventually gained over 70 pounds, it's pretty clear he just switched drugs from alcohol to

---

[11] Lorrain DS, et. al. Lateral Hypothalamic Serotonin Inhibits Nucleus Accumbens Dopamine: Implications for Sexual Satiety. The Journal of Neuroscience, September 1, 1999, 19(17):7648-7652.

overeating, but as the psychiatrist was taught that being obese is a different disease from alcoholism, he couldn't see this. The psychiatrist chased his symptoms for a couple of years, switching anti-depressants and raising their doses. While I think participation in AA would have helped, the patient wasn't able to maintain his AA involvement, perhaps because the lowered dopamine made him irritable and unable to concentrate. When he eventually came to see me, I explained to him how I saw what happened. Just that explanation helped because he had believed that he was beyond help as he had had a good psychiatrist who prescribed good medicines that worked for a little while. He thought he would not be able to recover in AA because something was wrong with him that wasn't wrong with other alcoholics; he thought he just "couldn't get it." I started him on a medicine to raise dopamine tone, and he began to feel better. After some coaxing he went back to AA, and this time those other people weren't so annoying and hard to understand. We eventually tapered the serotonin antidepressant. He's done well since and eventually even gotten off the dopamine medicine as his participation in AA has, I think, given him enough dopamine receptors to feel better. This is not an unusual case. I see this all the time. It's a shame that the people who could have taught the man's psychiatrist a different view either didn't know themselves or were afraid to speak it. Compromise and politics have a role in life, a big one. But when we're dealing with a force of nature, like a disease that neither knows nor cares what we want, compromise has very little role.

21. If this is so biological, why should I to go to AA? (or the 12-step group of your choice)

It's precisely because addiction is biological and permanent that a recovering addict should be involved in a 12-step program. One of my favorite studies answers for me why people with addiction benefit biologically from working a 12-step program. The study involves four normal infant monkeys. When offered cocaine these monkeys didn't like it and wouldn't continue using. Then the researchers took these young monkeys away from their mothers and put them in cages by themselves where they couldn't see any other monkeys. Like us, monkeys are social primates and like company. Being alone was very stressful. When they did a brain PET scan, they found the monkeys had fewer dopamine receptors than they had before. That means that in spite of the normal level of dopamine the monkeys had, they could not feel the dopamine signal as much as before. Now that they had a lowered dopamine tone, these monkeys also started to like cocaine and used it avidly. So they raised these monkeys in cages by themselves using cocaine until they were old enough to go in with other monkeys.

When the monkeys got to the right age, all four were put in a large group cage, and, of course, being monkeys, the first thing they did was compete to find out who was the alpha male monkey.

The winner was the big shot. He got more space, more food, and the others always backed off from him. So far that's what you'd expect from monkeys, but here's the kicker. The alpha male monkey stopped using cocaine, and when they PET scanned him, he had returned to a normal dopamine receptor density. The other three subservient monkeys continued to use cocaine and continued to have decreased dopamine receptor density.

So what do I learn from that study? That the stress of being alone and the stress of feeling less than someone else are the same stress to our primate brain; that they will both cause a decrease in dopamine receptor density; and that they will both cause the use of anything we have available to increase the dopamine reward signal. What do you get from 12-step programs? Two of the gifts of working a 12-step recovery program are that you come to know that you need never be alone again and that you aren't any less than anyone else. I've seen this work very quickly too.

You'll meet lots of people who say, "I knew when I walked into the meeting I was just going through the motions, and I was going to use when the meeting was over. But by the end of the meeting I was okay and I didn't use." You'll also meet people who were shamed by others and almost immediately sensed that the joy had gone out of life and started craving. So I think our dopamine receptor density can move up and down fairly quickly, and it's a biological change that I can't produce with medicine.

22. Is there any medical way to raise your dopamine receptor density?

Yes, there is. Recent studies[12] have been done where the gene for the dopamine receptor has been injected into the Medial Forebrain Bundle of a rodent that shows a preference for alcohol. The dopamine receptor gene turns out more dopamine receptors, the level rises, and the animal stops drinking as much alcohol.

So what's the catch? The effect doesn't last; it works for about 10 days. So if you're looking for an easier softer way than being honest with yourself and going to AA meetings, all you have to do is get a brain injection every 10 days. And if that sounds like a good idea, then you can still hear your disease talking to you.

---

[12] Thanos P, Volkow N, et al. Overexpression of Dopamine D2 Receptors Reduces Alcohol Self-administration. Journal of Neurochemistry 78(5); 2001:1094-1103.

23. If this is Addiction, what's Chemical Dependence?

For years and years the word dependence meant that if you stopped the substance you'd go into withdrawal. That's a normal human thing. Everyone who takes an opiate or most sedatives everyday will, if they stop suddenly, go into withdrawal. That doesn't mean they have addiction. In fact, most people will have withdrawal from some medications such as serotonin raising anti-depressants that no one would use to get high. Physical dependence has very little to do with addiction.

But addiction doesn't sound very medical and neither does alcoholism. I'm sure that at some point the insurance companies told doctors, "We don't pay for Communism or Judaism and we're not paying for Alcoholism." Well, doctors like to be paid, so they had to come up with another word. Unfortunately, they chose dependence, a word that already had a meaning. To confuse matters, they made withdrawal one of the symptoms of the new diagnosis Substance Dependence[13]. So, in essence, they took a word that meant something and said it means something else that the old word is potentially a part of. Could you understand that sentence the first three times you read it? Me either.

---

[13] Diagnostic and Statistical Manual of Mental Disorder (Third Edition). American Psychiatric Association, Washington DC, 1980.

So you can see why this is so confusing. Look back at question 17 to understand the biology of withdrawal as it relates to the biology of addiction. If you are drinking alcohol or taking opiates, it will seem to you and all those around you that withdrawal is part of addiction. But if you're using cocaine, you don't get tolerance and withdrawal. If you are overeating or gambling, it's not clear that you get withdrawal either. So you can probably see why I like the word addiction better than dependence. Substance Dependence makes it sound like the problem is the substance when in fact the problem is the brain. If you stop drinking alcohol but start overeating to get more dopamine, is that two illnesses? No, I don't think so, but using the term Substance Dependence makes it sound like it is.

24. Drugs or behaviors: what do we call these things?

It's kind of hard to come to terms with the words we need to use because all of the words already have a meaning to people. For instance, it makes no sense to call gambling a drug because it's obviously a behavior. To call taking cocaine a behavior is confusing because it mixes up the drug with the action of taking it. So we need to come up with a word or a phrase that means, in essence, stuff that releases dopamine. Science already has a term for that in behavioral psychology. The word is "reinforcer." Reinforcer doesn't really do it for me, but if you like that word for what we're talking about, I can live with it. My problem is that for behavioral scientists it brings up the idea that the person is normal and that no illness exists. The word I like better is "reward." A reward causes dopamine to be released in the reward center of the brain. It doesn't tell us if the reward comes from outside or inside, and it doesn't tell us if the person is ill or well. It's just a reward.

Now we can see that if people have normal reward systems and get normal reward from normal life, there is no need for other external reward inputs. However, if someone doesn't have a normal reward system and needs a specific behavior or drug to feel normal reward, then we will see their focus concentrate on that useful reward.

It might be helpful to know what sort of things give us a reward signal. For people with addiction these things can become compulsive. These include alcohol and drugs, of course, including nicotine. As well there is food[14] and sex. Interestingly, novel stimuli also work[15] and that would include 30 new images every second like TV or a video game. While I believe addiction is a single disease, people point out to me all the time the differences between addicts such as cocaine addicts and compulsive overeaters. "You don't see people grinding up hamburger and injecting it," they say with a smile to tell me how wrong I am. The difference is that different drugs and behaviors effect the reward system through different mechanisms. For instance cocaine works directly in the MFB to block the reuptake of dopamine (it blocks the vacuum cleaner raising the dopamine level) while food works through several different sensory mechanisms to release dopamine[16].

---

[14] Wise RA. Role of Brain Dopamine in Food Reward and Reinforcement. Philos Trans R Soc Lond B Biol Sci. 2006 Jul 29; 361(1471):1149-58.
[15] Knutson B, Cooper JC. The Lure of the Unknown. Neuron 2006 Aug 3; 51(3):280-2.
[16] Norgren R, Hajnal A, Mungarndee SS. Gustatory Reward and the Nucleus Accumbens. Physiol Behav. 2006 Nov 30;89(4):531-5.

25. Are drugs different from other rewards?

Well, that's the real question, isn't it? If addiction is limited to drugs, then drugs should be different from other rewards. But if research shows that drugs aren't different from other rewards, it makes it hard to see how addiction with drugs is different from addiction with any other reward.

In 2004[17] a group of researchers used micro-electronics to monitor anywhere from one to four brain cells inside the Nucleus Accumbens of rats that were exposed to rewards. They used both cocaine and water.

How can water be a reward? Remember this system didn't evolve to enjoy cocaine; it evolved to ensure the survival of the individual. When you're thirsty, water is supposed to be pretty rewarding. Otherwise we wouldn't drink it.

They found two interesting things. Both water and cocaine showed the same firing pattern in the Nucleus Accumbens, and, perhaps more interestingly, that different cells inside the Nucleus Accumbens responded to cocaine than those that responded to water. So it seems like the brain sets aside a few neurons that respond to one drug or another, but the firing pattern in the Nucleus Accumbens is the same regardless of the reward used.

---

[17] Deadwyler SA, et al. Reward, Memory and Substance Abuse: Functional Neuronal Circuits in the Nucleus Accumbens. Neuroscience and Biobehavioral Reviews, 2004; 27: 703-711.

Other researchers found that food, water, and sugar gave a similar pattern of response.[18] Still others[19] showed that while the patterns in the Nucleus Accumbens response is the same when cocaine and heroin are compared, the cells that responded differed just the way they did when cocaine was compared to water.

So difference in rewards doesn't really seem to matter, and that makes sense if you think in evolutionary terms. Would we end up designed to respond to drugs that haven't been invented yet or come from plants that don't grow where we live? Not likely. However, we need to be able to know what's good for us and to do those things that are good for us without thinking about them. We need to drink when we're thirsty and eat when we're hungry, and we need to be able to do those things automatically so that we don't have to spend a lot of time thinking about whether we should do them or not. That's why the Nucleus Accumbens does what it does, not so that people can get high on drugs. The reward system is there so that we can find things rewarding and do them unconsciously. Unfortunately, some of us don't have reward systems that work right for one reason or another, so we don't get rewarded by the little things. For that group it takes a bigger signal

---

[18] Carelli RM. Nucleus Accumbens Cell Firing During Goal-directed Behaviors for Cocaine vs "Natural" Reinforcement. Physiology and Behavior, 2002;76:379-387.

[19] Chang JY, Janak PH, Woodward DJ. Comparisons of Mesocorticolimbic Neuronal Responses During Cocaine and Heroin Self-administration in Freely Moving Rats. Journal of Neuroscience, 1998; 18: 3098-3115.

and the things that give us the signal are that much more important because the signal is all the more rare.

26. Can you put all the neurobiology stuff together in one picture along with what can go wrong?

Boy, you don't ask for much, do you? Okay, I'll describe it and try to draw a picture.

First, the basics of addiction are the inability to stop or moderate the reward when using and, when not using, to be constantly thinking about the reward and highly prone to using. There are three parts of the brain that bear on these two characteristics:

1. the dopamine/enkephalin feedback loop in the MFB
2. the glutamine signal to the MFB that can trigger relapse
3. the Periaqueductal Gray that handles withdrawal.

In the MFB, dopamine is produced and the reward causes it to be released to act on the reward center. That dopamine release causes a release of enkephalins, which prompt a further dopamine release, and this goes around and around until the dopamine is exhausted. The reward center also sends a signal to the front part the brain that instills positive self-esteem. If the enkephalin part or the dopamine part doesn't work right, the reward center doesn't send that signal as well as it should. Other things besides dopamine release can affect the dopamine signal. If the dopamine receptor isn't up to par, the signal won't get through as well. If the dopamine transporter recycles the dopamine too fast, it won't be there long enough to produce a good signal. Other things can be wrong as well: don't make enough dopamine, don't get dopamine down to the end of the neuron, don't release enough dopamine in each packet, don't release enough packets with each reward, don't send the signal from the receptors, or don't transmit the signal to the frontal cortex. And you can increase the list by thinking of everything that can go wrong in the enkephalin part of the cycle as well.

If you don't have enough dopamine signal, you will not be able to concentrate; you will feel restless, irritable, and discontented. You may have low self-esteem and feel as if you don't fit into the world. Because you'll enjoy few regular activities, not much will motivate you and you'll have problems with procrastination and motivation. When you use the reward that works for you, your level will be high enough to feel normal and you'll stop using for a bit. When the level falls, the signal will actually go lower than it was when it started so that you'll feel compelled to use again. This is the basis of not being able to stop once started.

The glutamate signal to the MFB is more about triggering with cues and relapse. Anything can do it; a person, place, or thing is sufficient. Also a time of day, a weather pattern, or a news event are all things that could be a cue for a trigger. The glutamate signal sets off the MFB, and you get the drop in level even without using the reward. Once the level drops the person will feel compelled to use.

The Periaqueductal Gray handles withdrawal and since we use drugs systemically, taking a drug while in withdrawal will calm the symptoms. The PG does have a connection with the MFB that causes the dopamine level to fall, just like hunger or thirst would. That's what lets us know it's the drug we need to stop the withdrawal.

Sorry, but you'll have to turn the book sideways to see the picture.

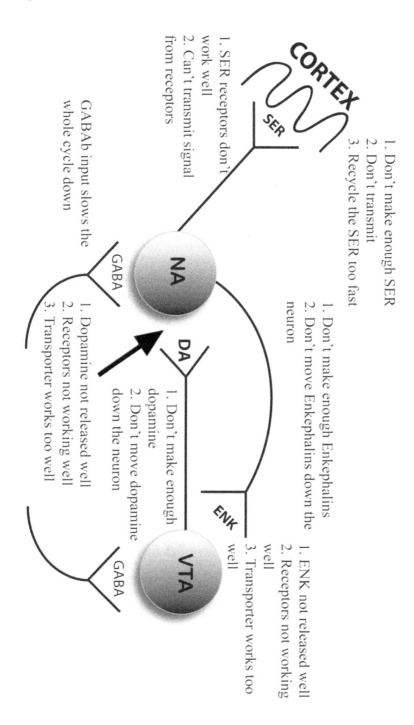

27. Does neurobiology also determine who likes which reward?

Yes, I believe so. Let's take a look at a recent article published in the prestigious Journal of Addiction Medicine. Han, Lee, et al published a study[20] done on over 140 Korean male adolescents, about half of whom had what the authors called "Excessive Internet Game Play (EIGP)." What they found was that the boys with EIGP were more likely to have a mutation of one of their dopamine receptors that made it more difficult to see the dopamine signal. They also found that for the kids with EIGP, the dopamine receptor mutation was associated with a measure of reward dependence that sort of corresponds with the Cloninger Type II I told you about. Well, that makes sense from what I've told you so far.

What's surprising is that the EIGP kids were also more likely to have a mutation of their enzyme that breaks down dopamine (COMT), leading to a higher dopamine spike with a reward. Well, that doesn't make sense at first, but let's think about it. Say you have low dopamine tone and you play a video game and get a normal person's reward from it – well, no big deal. But if

---

[20] Han DH, Lee YS, et al. Dopamine Genes and Reward Dependence in Adolescents with Excessive Internet Video Game Play. JAM 1 (3), Sep 2007; 133-138.

you got a better than normal reward from it because you also had the COMT mutation the game would be much more rewarding. In essence what the researchers found was that the dopamine receptor problem was the set up and the ability to have a bigger than normal release with such a little response was what made the kids respond to video games. Perhaps you don't need that COMT mutation to respond to stronger stimulants, such as cocaine. This is an example where two problems pool together to make a specific reward more likely to be used.

You can look at the diagram on page 72 and think about other examples. What if your dopamine function is fine, but your enkephalin receptor is broken. You won't feel normal levels of reward unless you have an opiate in your system. But maybe cocaine won't work so well because your dopamine system is fine for now. Anything you can imagine that could go wrong in the diagram has probably been done in nature. In the future we'll have the ability to look at the genes in this system so that we can more accurately pinpoint the treatment.

28. What are the medications used in Addiction?

GABA Receptor Agents: There are two reasons for using a medicine that turns on the GABA receptor. The first is to make withdrawal from sedatives and alcohol easier. The second is to get a special effect on the dopamine spike.

For withdrawal, we use the drugs that were originally designed to combat epileptic seizures. I'll call them Anti-epilepsy Drugs (AEDs). There are several AEDs and most are equally as good in making sedative withdrawal better, but the one I like the best for that purpose is valproic acid, sometimes called valproate. Many of the newer medications have to have the dosage slowly built up over time, so it doesn't do much good if you're in withdrawal. With valproate we can start the full dose in the first day and get some relief. Another one that works fast and is therefore good for withdrawal is a medicine called carbamazepine.

The other reason to use an agent that acts positively at the GABA receptor is to use one that specifically turns on a particular type of GABA receptor called GABAb. Under the influence of GABAb the dopamine spike from a drug is not as high and the resulting crash is not as low. It can help someone who is trying to stop using from using as much as they had been. There's no guarantee with it, but it's a useful technique. The AEDs are good for this GABAb effect as well as an old muscle relaxant called baclofen. We don't need to use this as much as we used to now that acamprosate is available in this country (see glutamate agents below).

Dopamine Agents: If the problem is that there is not enough dopamine tone and because of that normally rewarding things are not rewarding, we can raise the dopamine tone. Hopefully then the person can feel reward from normally rewarding events and not have to look for external rewards to get to a normal level. There are a few ways to do this. My favorite is to block the reuptake of dopamine with a drug called buproprion, but only the long acting version. Another is to stimulate the release of dopamine with a new drug called varenicline. Varenicline works at the nicotine receptor to release dopamine. It's been approved by the FDA to help people stop smoking and it's pretty new.

There are a couple of other medications that other doctors use that I have not found helpful in the long run in treating people with addiction. The first is amphetamines, and the second is a drug called modafinil. Amphetamines are dangerous because they don't just block the reuptake of dopamine, they run the reuptake pump in reverse. At first it was thought that modafinil worked like buproprion, and only blocked the reuptake of dopamine. But I've had a couple of patients report it felt and acted more like an amphetamine, so I've stopped using it.

Glutamate Modulators: A new medication called acamprosate works to block the glutamate-triggered craving that comes in response to sensory cues that remind the person of previous drug use. The glutamate signal is normally released in the reward center and serves to get the compulsive use cycle spinning. Because each dopamine spike is followed by a crash, this spinning leads to the craving one normally feels during the dopamine crash. With acamprosate blocking the glutamate signal, the reward circuit doesn't spin up as much, and there is less chance of craving.

I've also noticed that it helps with what we used to call "denial" and now call "pre-contemplation." I think the denial is caused by an overflow of the brain's opioids into the area that remembers emotions, and under the influence of this overflow the person cannot remember how bad it was to use. As the acamprosate tunes down the glutamate signal, the reward system doesn't get spun up. So, instead of the brain's opioids flooding the area and causing "denial," acamprosate keeps the opioid flood from happening. It's been very helpful and low in side effects.

Since using acamprosate, I have not had the need to use a GABAb agent much other than for withdrawal. The GABAb effect must have been lowering glutamate but maybe not as directly because acamprosate seems to work better than the AEDs on the issue of denial.

Opioid Receptor Agents: A lot of doctors block the opioid receptor, which makes sense if you want to stop drug use. It doesn't make as much sense if you're treating what was wrong with the person before they started using drugs to feel better. The medication to block the opiate receptor is called naltrexone, and it has recently been released as a once a month shot for people who have had trouble maintaining abstinence.

A new drug called buprenorphine has been approved by the DEA and the FDA to treat opioid addiction. It gets on the opioid receptor and turns it on just enough to feel normal and not high. My patients have had a great deal of success with it. Buprenorphine can only be started once all the opioid the person has been using is out of his system, so it's a difficult drug to get on especially if the patient has been using methadone or another long acting opioid. But patients are on it they generally do very well.

29. Who needs more than medicine and recovery?

Imagine if you will someone with diabetes whose diabetes progresses to the point where they have to have their foot amputated or become blind. Now imagine that someone comes along with a treatment that gets their diabetes under control. We won't expect them to re-grow the foot or regain the sight just because the biology of the disease is under control. So it is with addiction as well. Once you're open to the idea that most people with addiction have the biology from birth, it becomes easy to understand that the biology of addiction has a profound effect on the personality of the person as they grow. They will make accommodations for the illness just as anyone else would. When the biology and the symptoms come under control, it takes time to learn to live without them.

That might sound strange, but there's an old vaudeville joke that illustrates the point. A man breaks his hand and goes to the doctor to get a cast. The man says, "Hey Doc, when this hand heals will I be able to play the violin?" "Sure," says the doctor, "No problem." "That's great," says the man, "'cause I never could before."

While anybody can see that someone who couldn't play the violin isn't going to be able to play simply because they get some medical treatment, we don't apply it to things we take for granted like forming relationships, being honest, and trusting the universe to provide. We figure everyone should be able to do those things without any learning, but it's not really so. The disease actively blocked a lot of learning about how life really works, and that learning has to happen even after the biological symptoms of the disease are suppressed. A lot of this learning takes place over time in a 12-step program, but several studies have shown that the addition of professional treatment improves the outcome.

So what kind of therapy is best? Well, that depends on several factors. Historically there are four reasons a patient should go to inpatient treatment or "rehab." First is to change the environment. When the patient lives where someone else is using or is unsupportive of his recovery, it is often best to change where the patient lives. Second, on a residential basis you can provide more treatment directly to the patient in a controlled and intensive way. A third reason is the availability of psychiatric consultation. This reason has really gone by the wayside because many outpatient facilities have psychiatrists now. The fourth reason is a bit of a stretch as well – the person will take it more seriously if they have to go to rehab away from home. Of course, if they refuse to go to inpatient treatment, taking it seriously doesn't help much. A 1996 study[21] showed that out of seven studies of the efficacy of

---

[21] Finney JW & Moos RH. Effectiveness of Inpatient and Outpatient Treatment for Alcohol Abuse: Effect Sizes, Research Design Issues, and Explanatory Mechanisms. Addiction 91:1813-1820.

inpatient treatment over outpatient treatment five showed that inpatient was better.

How long people stay in treatment has an effect as well. Even more important, a review of the relevant studies suggests that treatment is best done at a lower than daily intensity over a longer period of time.[22] So the ideal treatment is the one the patient is willing to commit to and engage in for the longest period. That really makes sense when you think about it. If this illness had quick fixes, wouldn't we have found them by now?

So if the only thing a patient is willing to do is see an outpatient therapist, that's better than nothing. However, groups work better than single therapists for addiction as people learn faster in a group. Intensive outpatient therapy where the patient is in treatment at least 3 hours a day, three or more times a week for more than 6 weeks with a prolonged aftercare is a good alternative and often cheaper than inpatient rehab.

---

[22] Finney JW and Moos RH. Effects of Setting, Duration, and Amount on Treatment Outcomes (Chapter 4, Section4, p448) in Principles of Addiction Medicine, American Society of Addiction Medicine, Washington DC 2003.

30. I got treatment, I'm taking medicine. So why do I need this recovery stuff too?

It would be nice if this illness was like strep throat. Get treated and it's gone. Even if strep throat left long lasting effects, like scarlet fever or a heart valve problem, the disease itself is gone. Unfortunately, addiction is not like strep throat. The medication we use to treat the illness, at best, suppresses the symptoms. The treatment, at best, corrects any non-reality based learning caused by the disease. And if the disease would just go away those benefits of medication and treatment would be enough. Sorry, the disease is not going to just go away.

Some of you are saying, "But wait a minute. My Uncle Bob got religion and just stopped drinking and did fine for the rest of his life." Yep, you're right, and everyone knows an Uncle Bob. I'm sure you can find several examples. But if everyone were like Uncle Bob, I could be doing something else for a living. I'm doing this because Uncle Bob is actually pretty rare, and as we'll discuss later, probably in recovery anyway, just in a different way.

So let's talk about what recovery is so we can know why we need to be doing it. Of course my view of recovery is colored by my bias of understanding this illness in a biological way. There are many people who see recovery in a lot of different ways, and I in no way mean to invalidate any of them. I hope you see by the end of this answer that it doesn't matter what words we're using to describe recovery, but that recovery is recovery. William White and others put together a monograph on recovery which is a much broader discussion than I'll have here.[23]

I guess I don't have to repeat here that there is more to recovery than just not using. There's also more to it than just not using and not having symptoms of low dopamine (irritable, not enjoying life, aloof). Not using and not having the symptoms of low dopamine are, hopefully, the end result of working a recovery program. They are the outcome, not the action itself. This concept is confusing to a lot of people I meet. It's kind of like wishing for cooler weather so you put your thermometer in the refrigerator. Nothing changes but the number on the thermometer. So as we discuss recovery, remember the difference between the thing itself and the measure of the outcome.

So what is recovery? Well, I've been putting this definition off for few paragraphs haven't I? It's time to take the bull by the horns and answer the question. Recovery, for this addiction doctor at least, is taking action in every moment of the day to minimize the feelings of aloneness and less-than that precipitate a lowering of our dopamine receptor density.

---

[23] White WL, Kurtz E, Sanders M. Recovery Management. Great Lakes Addiction Technology Transfer Center, Chicago, Il. 2006.

I can imagine many ways to do recovery and everyone else can to. And if all of these ways worked, again, I'd be doing something else for a living. So we have to go further. The actions we take actually have to be effective. Since millions of people have been in recovery in the past, we should have ample evidence as to what works and what doesn't. But we can even do better than that. We can find someone like us, someone who tells our story when he tells his own, but has found a way to live that gives him the happiness, freedom, and joy that we want. I'm betting that the actions he lives by will have better odds of success than a random set we could come up with on our own. If you have any experience with 12-step recovery, you've probably recognized the description of how to pick a sponsor. Even if you don't want to work a 12-step program, the idea is the same. You can maximize the odds of a good outcome by choosing someone who you can relate to, someone who has what you want, and then by following his path. Kind of a cop out for me, huh? I said I'd tell you what recovery is and then told you to get a sponsor. Now that I got that out of the way, here's what I think you'll hear from that sponsor.

In watching many people's recovery and in studying many philosophical and religious traditions, I think I see a commonality in what works. I've heard it expressed many ways: "Whenever I'm at the bottom of the hole, I'm the one holding the shovel," "We admitted we were powerless over our addiction – that our lives had become unmanageable," "It is a spiritual axiom that whenever we're disturbed, no matter what the cause, there's something wrong with us." The main point for me is a recognition that the brain with the illness is not going to think of a way to fix itself, and all attempts to do so will only make the problem worse. That means we need other people and a set of directions for life we can trust.

It's hard to trust others' brains more than you trust your own. Maybe that's why it often takes so long to get into good recovery. It's hard to decide not to trust your own brain and trust others instead. Navy pilots have good results in treatment and recovery; maybe that's because they're trained to believe the instruments and disregard their own sense of position. They already understand that the brain can't always be trusted. But it's hard to trust something other than our own brain. We don't walk around with a set of instruments like the pilots have. How do we find something to trust?

Well, it's pretty axiomatic that if we aren't going to trust our own brain we probably shouldn't trust anyone else's either. So I'm not advocating taking advice from other people. They can be just as wrong as you. We need a set of directions that transcend personal opinion. We need a set of directions that work and have worked for a long time. We surround ourselves not with people who will grace us with their opinions, but with people who will remind us of the directions that work. It's especially wonderful when they guide us without their own egos involved.

Now, I'd like to say something about one of those directions that you'll hear: help other people. It's amazing how powerful helping others is and how common to all programs of recovery. Think about it this way. We were alone, others helped us, and now we have to help others who are alone. I like the symmetry of that.

So there are some things in common we will see in any successful recovery program. It has to be that way because the only way recovery can work is to change the brain in a specific way to increase dopamine tone. And we know what increases dopamine receptors. So no matter what words we use to describe it, recovery will be recovery because it will have to do what's necessary to keep the brain changed in a positive way even though the disease won't go away.

First, there will be other people. That's a must. The other people will not be in charge but will be egoless transmitters of principles and directions that work in life, and one of those principles will be to help other people get what you got. These people won't be perfect because they won't be any better than you. So by practice they will be a forgiving lot and not prone to shaming others.

This is where the idea of a higher power comes in. It turns out it's pretty easy to feel ashamed when we compare something about us to another person. That's why other people don't work so well as higher powers. If you have the idea that what the directions are based on is larger than yourself, there's not much shame even when you fall short. This is true for higher powers as diverse as "the laws of physics" and "God." None of us can be as perfect as either of those ideals, so shame doesn't seem to enter the equation. That's another thing in common about different forms of recovery; the directions aren't going to be coming from the guy down the street or even from someone famous who died a while back. They'll be an expression of truth that is more timeless than what we can learn in a single lifetime. They'll be directions for living that have worked for every generation. No matter what the word is that you use to define your "power greater than ourselves," the directions will probably be the same.

So let's go back to Uncle Bob's religious conversion. Did Uncle Bob find religion and then go off by himself to live in a cave? I doubt it. More likely Uncle Bob belonged to a group of people who tried to follow a set of directions they themselves did not make up, and he engaged in acting on those directions with the help of those people. I'm betting that at least one of the directions was to help others. I'm also betting that they were a forgiving bunch and had rules about cutting themselves and others some slack when they fell short of the ideal. Remember, they are trying not to feel less than other people.

It is the amazingly optimistic conclusion that flows from the commonality of recovery that I'll end with. Even though the disease won't go away, even though it gets worse with time, if we join with and follow the directions that have worked for others like us we can be happy, joyous, and free.

31. I know you said you were finished, but I have one last question: could you be wrong?

Of course I could be. Science is always making new discoveries. I didn't know any of this 10 years ago, and if this is all I know 10 years from now, I'll be real disappointed. If any of this is wrong, the best thing is to find out, and when I do, I'll change it in the next edition